EDIBLE GIFTS

Consultant Editor:
Valerie Ferguson

southwater

Contents

Introduction

Few gifts are more appreciated than those that have been made by the giver. It is also very satisfying to make something yourself for someone you love. Hand-made truffles or fudge are so much more special than ordinary chocolates and a pretty bottle of a traditional country cordial makes a thoughtful and unusual gift.

This book is packed with recipes for all kinds of edible gifts from preserves to candies and from spiced oils to chutneys. There are delicious treats for the sweet-toothed; unusual cheeses; savoury butters and mustards; luxurious jams and jellies, delicious drinks and even an edible chocolate box!

A helpful introduction gives advice about preparing and sterilizing jars and bottles, as well as suggesting clever presentation ideas to give your gifts a personal touch. Basic techniques for making preserves and melting chocolate are also included.

Making edible gifts does not have to be immensely time-consuming and costly. However, forward planning is sometimes essential, as flavours may need to infuse or mature. Whether you are giving at Christmas or a birthday, as a thank you or just to say "I love you", you will find the perfect present here.

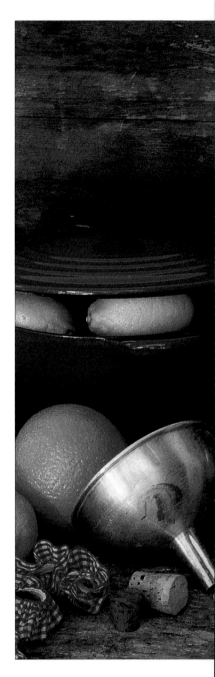

Techniques

Sterilizing Containers

Clear glass jars are ideal for jams and jellies and can also be used for chutneys and mustards. These also look attractive in earthenware containers. Clear bottles are a good choice for cordials and flavoured oils and vinegars. Whichever you choose, make sure that there are no cracks or chips and that the container has been thoroughly washed in hot soapy water and rinsed well. Wash and rinse any lids or stoppers.

An easy way to sterilize bottles in particular is with sterilizing tablets. These are available from chemists and winemaking suppliers. Make a solution in water according to the packet instructions. Pour it into the bottles through a funnel and leave for the specified time. Soak stoppers in a Campden solution.

There are a number of ways of sterilizing jars for preserves. To do it in the oven, stand the jars on a baking sheet lined with newspaper or on a wooden board. Rest any lids on the jars but do not seal. Put them in a cold oven, set to 110°C/225°F/Gas ¼ and leave for 30 minutes. The advantage of this method is that it ensures the containers are dry and warm, so that the glass is unlikely to crack when hot jam or chutney is ladled in.

Jars can also be sterilized in a dishwasher on its hottest setting, with the drying cycle. Do not use detergent.

Jelly bags should also be sterilized. Set the bag over a large bowl and pour boiling water through, then discard the water and replace with a clean bowl.

Seals

The surface of jams and jellies can be covered with a disc of greaseproof paper and the jar covered with paper or cellophane held in place with an elastic band. Chutneys and pickles should always be sealed with vinegar-proof lids to prevent corrosion. Bottled fruits and vegetables are best in proper preserving jars fitted with new rubber seals and the lids clipped in place. Any bottles that do not have glass stoppers should be sealed with new corks.

Labels

Decorative self-adhesive labels are widely available. Alternatively, wooden or metal labels may be tied around the neck of the container. Preserves should always be labelled with a description of their contents and the date.

Blanching Herbs
There is evidence that oils containing fresh herbs can develop harmful moulds. Blanch the herbs briefly and shake dry before using.

Setting Point
The most reliable way to check for setting point is to use a sugar thermometer. When the temperature reaches 105°C/221°F, the jam is ready. Otherwise, test by spooning a small quantity of the mixture on to a chilled saucer. Chill for 3 minutes, then push the surface with your finger. If it wrinkles, the jam is at setting point. If you leave the jam to stand for about 15 minutes before ladling into jars, the fruit will be more evenly distributed.

Melting Chocolate in a Double Boiler
This is probably the most traditional method of melting chocolate.

1 If you do not have a double boiler, place a small heatproof bowl over a saucepan. Make sure it fits snugly so no water or steam can splash into it. The water in the base should be barely simmering.

2 Place broken chocolate in the double boiler top or bowl and set it in place. Lower the heat or turn it off completely, and melt the chocolate slowly, stirring frequently.

Melting Chocolate over Direct Heat
When a recipe requires that chocolate should be melted with a liquid such as cream, it can safely be done over direct heat in a saucepan.

1 Place the chocolate and liquid in a heavy-based saucepan over a low heat. Stir frequently until the chocolate is melted and smooth. Remove from the heat immediately.

2 Chocolate can also be melted in a very low oven (about 110°C/225°F/ Gas ¼). Put the chocolate in an ovenproof bowl and place in the oven for a few minutes. Put the timer on so that you do not forget it. Remove the chocolate from the oven before it is completely melted and stir with a wooden spoon until smooth.

Crystallized Flowers
Brush flowers and leaves, such as roses, pansies, violas, herb flowers and variegated mint, with raw egg white and sprinkle with caster sugar. Leave to dry for 1-2 hours on a plate or rack out of direct sunlight. Use on the day of making.

Presentation Ideas

The finishing touches can make your edible gift really special.

Above: Herbs and leaves make excellent decorations for a jar.

Jars of preserves look more attractive decorated. Tie an autumn leaf, a sprig of flowers or a bunch of fresh herbs to the neck or lid with raffia, ribbon or twine. A bunch of chillies would provide a colourful touch on a bottle of chilli oil or jar of chutney. The tops of jars

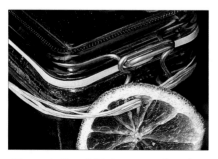

Above: A slice of dried orange makes an eloquent label on a jar of marmalade.

can also be covered with a circle of pretty fabric over the cellophane cover

Sweets and biscuits look twice as appetizing nestling neatly in a box. There are many different boxes in a wide range of designs, colours and sizes available from stationers and department stores. Alternatively, you could cover a plain box with wrapping paper or fabric, or pack biscuits in a decorative tin. These are often sold for storing pens and pencils, but make excellent airtight containers.

Above: Try packing a selection of gifts in a straw-lined basket.

Gift bags, available in a range of sizes, are ideal for awkwardly shaped items, such as cheeses or pâté. They often have matching gift tags.

Unusual or particularly attractive earthenware, glass or china containers make a gift of pâté or savoury butter even more special and remain a permanent reminder when the original contents have been consumed

Sweets & Biscuits

If your gift will be presented, and consumed, relatively quickly, and the contents do not need to be stored in an airtight container, then a pretty box lined with tissue paper may be the ideal solution.

1 Line your chosen container with three or four sheets of co-ordinating tissue paper. After positioning the first piece of paper, lay the others on top, alternating the corners to fill the spaces. Crumpled tissue paper has a charm all its own. You may wish to crumple it first, then lightly smooth it out.

2 Carefully place the contents inside the box, and fold the excess tissue paper over the top for extra security before replacing the lid.

Marzipan Fruits

Fruits sculpted from marzipan always look so delightful that it's a shame to hide them away in a box.

1 Choose a transparent container to show the fruits to best effect. This one is very simple in design, but you may wish to choose a more elaborate, glass container. Carefully position the fruits inside the container.

2 Finish with a co-ordinating ribbon or decoration, secured to the lid with double-sided tape.

Potted Spreads & Butters

Spreads and flavoured butters are particularly enchanting when they are packed in little jars.

1 Decorate the top with ribbon curls in suitable colours (you may want to reflect the colours of the contents of the jars). Fix the ribbon curls in place with double-sided tape.

2 If you wish to present several assorted jars, try packing them together in a bag made of decorative wrapping paper.

Strawberry Jam

This classic recipe is always popular. Make sure the jam is allowed to cool before pouring into jars so the fruit doesn't float to the top.

Makes about 2.25 kg/5 lb

INGREDIENTS
1.5 kg/3–3½ lb strawberries
juice of ½ lemon
1.5 kg/3–3½ lb granulated sugar

1 Hull the strawberries. Put the strawberries in a pan with the lemon juice. Mash a few of the strawberries. Simmer the fruit for 20 minutes, or until softened.

2 Add the sugar and dissolve it slowly over a gentle heat. Then bring the jam to the boil and boil rapidly until a setting point is reached.

3 Leave to stand until the strawberries are well distributed through the jam. Ladle into sterilized jars. Seal, label and store in a cool dark place. The jam may be kept unopened for up to a year. Once the jars are opened, keep in the fridge and consume within 1 week.

Lemon & Mint Curd

Home-made lemon curd is infinitely tastier than the commercial variety. The addition of mint gives this version an interesting extra tang.

Makes about 1.5 kg/3–3½ lb

INGREDIENTS
6 fresh mint leaves
900 g/2 lb/4½ cups caster sugar
350 g/12 oz/1½ cups butter, cut into chunks
rind and juice of 6 lemons
8 eggs, beaten

1 Place the mint leaves and sugar in a food processor and blend until the mint leaves are very finely chopped and combined with the sugar.

2 Put the mint sugar and all the other ingredients into a bowl and mix together thoroughly.

3 Set the bowl over a saucepan of simmering water. Cook, whisking the mixture gently, until all the butter has melted and the sugar has completely dissolved. Remove the pieces of lemon rind.

4 Continue to cook in this way, stirring frequently, for 35–40 minutes, or until the mixture thickens.

5 Ladle the lemon mixture into sterilized glass jars, filling them right up to the rim. Seal, label and tie short lengths of string around the top of the jars to decorate. This lemon curd should be used within 3 months.

Lavender Jelly

This is a wonderfully fragrant jelly which captures the essence of summer. It is as versatile as it is lovely and can be served with lamb and smoked chicken or eaten with croissants and scones.

Makes 1.8 kg/4 lb

INGREDIENTS
1.8 kg/4 lb cooking apples, chopped
90 ml/6 tbsp lavender flowers
1.75 litres/3 pints/7½ cups water
1.3 kg/3 lb/6¾ cups sugar

1 Simmer the apples with 75 ml/ 5 tbsp lavender flowers and the water until soft and mushy. Put in a jelly bag and let drip for several hours.

COOK'S TIP: Lavender often flowers for a second time in autumn when cooking apples are ripening, so it is good to make this at that time of year.

2 Measure the resulting liquid and allow 450 g/1 lb/2¼ cups sugar to each 600 ml/1 pint/2½ cups of liquid. Place the sugar and fruit liquid in a large heavy-based saucepan and gradually bring to the boil until setting point is reached.

3 Remove the liquid from the heat and allow it to cool for 20 minutes. Skim off any scum carefully with a slotted spoon.

4 Stir in the remaining lavender flowers and then ladle the jelly into small warm sterilized jars (use the prettiest ones you can find). Seal and label the jars.

Dried-fruit Rumtopf

This wonderfully rich and fruity preserve should be stored for at least four weeks to allow the flavours to blend. For a quick and easy dessert, serve decorated with an orange slice and a sprig of fresh mint.

Makes about 1.2 kg/2½ lb

INGREDIENTS
115 g/4 oz/½ cup granulated sugar
250 ml/8 fl oz/1 cup water
225 g/8 oz/2 cups dried apricots,
  soaked and drained
225 g/8 oz/2 cups dried
  apricot halves
115 g/4 oz/⅔ cup stoned prunes
115 g/4 oz/⅔ cup semi-dried figs
115 g/4 oz/½ cup dried apple rings
225 g/8 oz/1 cup dried orange rings
5 ml/1 tsp cloves
3 sticks cinnamon, halved
about 350 ml/12 fl oz/1½ cups dark rum
  or brandy

1 Put the sugar and water in a pan over a low heat. Stir until the sugar has dissolved, then bring to the boil and boil, without stirring, for 5 minutes. Set aside to cool.

2 Pack the fruit into three dry, sterilized 450 g/1 lb jars, arranging in layers. Divide the cloves, cinnamon sticks and syrup among the jars and top up with rum or brandy, making sure to cover the fruit.

3 Cover and seal the jars and tip from side to side to blend the liquids. Cool completely, then label and store in a cool place for up to 6 months.

Orange Marmalade

Marmalade has been made with Seville oranges for over 500 years and these are still the most suitable.

Makes about 4 kg/9½ lb

INGREDIENTS
1 kg/2¼ lb Seville oranges
1 lemon
2.2 litres/4 pints/9 cups water
1.8 kg/4 lb preserving sugar

1 Quarter the oranges and lemon. Remove the flesh from all the fruit and tie in a piece of muslin. Slice the rind finely or coarsely according to taste.

2 Place the rind and the muslin bag in a preserving pan or large saucepan and add the water. Bring to the boil, then lower the heat and simmer for 1½–2 hours, until the rind is tender.

3 Meanwhile, warm the sugar in a low oven. Stir the sugar into the marmalade until it has dissolved, then boil it rapidly until setting point is reached.

4 Remove the muslin bag. Set aside for 15 minutes, then ladle the marmalade into warm, sterilized jars. Cover and label.

Flavoured Honeys

The finest honeys are those which are made by bees collecting from a single flower source, such as clover, lime blossom or wild thyme.

Makes 450 g/1 lb

INGREDIENTS
VANILLA HONEY
1 vanilla pod
450 g/1 lb clear honey

GINGER HONEY
1 piece stem ginger, sliced
450 g/1 lb clear honey

WHISKY HONEY
450 g/1 lb set honey
45 ml/3 tbsp whisky

1 For vanilla honey, immerse the vanilla pod in the jar of honey. Leave to stand for 1 week, stirring occasionally. Remove the vanilla pod.

2 For ginger honey, stir the stem ginger into the honey. Leave to stand for 1 week, stirring occasionally. Use it for a honey-and-lemon drink.

3 For whisky honey, gently heat the jar of honey in a pan of simmering water. Add the whisky, stir to mix and allow to reset.

Aromatic Spiced Peaches

A great gift for friends who hate cooking, this indulgent dessert is superb served with vanilla ice cream, honey and chopped stem ginger.

Makes about 1 kg/2¼ lb

INGREDIENTS
300 ml/½ pint/1¼ cups water
500 g/1¼ lb/2½ cups granulated sugar
12 peaches
2 cinnamon sticks
4 star anise
300 ml/½ pint/1¼ cups brandy

1 Pour the water into a saucepan, add the sugar and heat gently, stirring, until dissolved. Bring to the boil and boil for 2 minutes, without stirring.

COOK'S TIP: You may find the fruit will rise to begin with but, as it becomes saturated with the syrup, it will sink back to the bottom.

2 Halve and stone the peaches and halve the cinnamon sticks. Add the peaches, cinnamon and star anise to the syrup, return to the boil, then cover and simmer for 5 minutes, turning the peaches once or twice.

3 Lift the peaches out with a slotted spoon and pack into two warm, dry, sterilized jars. Divide the spices among the two jars. Boil the remaining sugar syrup rapidly for 5 minutes and pour into the jars to half-fill them.

4 Top up with brandy, making sure the fruit is covered. Add a piece of crumpled greaseproof paper on top and seal well. Cool completely, then store in a cool dark place for up to 6 months before opening.

Kumquats & Limequats in Brandy Syrup

These brightly coloured fruits taste very good served with thick creamy yogurt or spooned over vanilla ice cream.

Makes about 450 g/1 lb

INGREDIENTS
450 g/1 lb kumquats and limequats
175 g/6 oz/¾ cup granulated sugar
300 ml/½ pint/1¼ cups water
150 ml/¼ pint/⅔ cup brandy
15 ml/1 tbsp orange flower water

1 Using a toothpick, prick each individual fruit in several places. Put the sugar in the water and heat gently, stirring, until the sugar has dissolved.

2 Bring to the boil, then add the fruit and simmer, without stirring, for about 25 minutes, until the fruit is tender.

3 Drain the fruit and spoon into hot, dry, sterilized jars. The syrup should be fairly thick: if not, boil for a few minutes, then allow to cool slightly. Stir in the brandy and the orange flower water, pour over the fruit and seal the jars immediately. Store the preserved fruit in a cool place and use within 6 months.

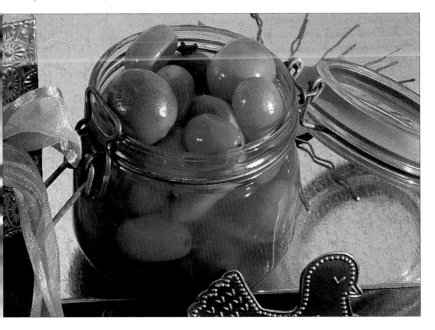

Elderflower Cordial

This makes a wonderfully refreshing summer drink or a delicious sorbet and gives a subtle flavour when added to cooked gooseberries.

Makes 2.5 litres/
4¼ pints/10¼ cups

INGREDIENTS
1.5 kg/3½ lb/8 cups
   granulated sugar
1.5 litres/2½ pints/6¼ cups
   hot water
50 g/2 oz citric acid
25 elderflower heads, washed and gently
   shaken dry
2 lemons, sliced

1 Dissolve the sugar in the water and set aside to cool. When cool, stir in the citric acid and add the elderflowers and lemons. Cover and leave to infuse for 2 days, stirring occasionally.

2 Strain and pour into clean, dry sterilized bottles, seal and label. Store in a cool dark place.

3 To serve, pour the cordial into glasses and dilute to taste with still or sparkling mineral water.

Right: Elderberry Syrup (left);
Elderflower Cordial

Elderberry Syrup

Elderberries are ripe when the heads hang down. This is a traditional country remedy for coughs and colds.

Makes about 750 ml/1¼ pints/
3 cups

INGREDIENTS
ripe elderberries
granulated sugar
cinnamon sticks

1 Preheat the oven to 190°C/375°F/ Gas 5. Wash the heads of the elderberries thoroughly, remove the stalks and then place the berries in a large, earthenware pot. Cover and bake until the juice runs.

2 Strain off the elderberry juice and measure, then pour into a saucepan. For each 600 ml/1 pint/2½ cups juice, add 225 g/8 oz/generous 1 cup granulated sugar and a broken up cinnamon stick.

3 Cover the pan and bring to the boil over a low heat. Boil gently until the syrup thickens.

4 Pour the syrup into warm, dry sterilized bottles, seal securely and label. To serve, dilute to taste with hot water.

Rosehip Cordial

If you get the chance to collect rosehips from the hedgerows, this cordial makes a wonderful Christmas present.

Makes 1.75 litres/
3 pints/7½ cups

INGREDIENTS
2.5 litres/4½ pints/10¼ cups water
1 kg/2¼ lb/6 cups rosehips
450 g/1 lb/2¼ cups granulated sugar

1 Bring 1.75 litres/3 pints/7½ cups water to the boil in a large heavy-based saucepan. Put the rosehips in a food processor and process until finely chopped. Add to the boiling water, bring back to the boil, cover and turn off the heat. Leave to infuse for 15 minutes.

2 Suspend a jelly bag and place a bowl underneath. Sterilize the jelly bag by pouring boiling water through it, then discard the water and replace the bowl.

3 Strain the rosehips through the jelly bag and leave them to drip until the pulp is almost dry.

4 Return the pulp to the saucepan with another 900 ml/1½ pints/3¾ cups water, bring to the boil, cover and infuse for 10 minutes as above and strain, mixing the two juices together.

5 Pour the juices back into a clean saucepan and boil to reduce the mixture by half, to about 1 litre/1¾ pints/4 cups. Stir in the sugar, heat gently until dissolved, then boil for 5 minutes.

6 Pour the cordial into warm, sterilized bottles, seal securely and label. Store in the fridge. If the cordial is to be kept for longer than four weeks, sterilize before bottling by adding one crushed Campden tablet dissolved in 15 ml/1 tbsp boiling water to each 600 ml/1 pint/2½ cups cordial.

VARIATION: If rosehips are not available, you can make a delicious cordial from blackcurrants instead.

Peach Wine

This is not strictly a wine, but a delicious and refreshing amalgam of peaches, wine and eau de vie.

Makes about 1.2 litres/
2 pints/5 cups

INGREDIENTS
6 ripe peaches, peeled, halved
    and stoned
1 litre/1¾ pints/4 cups dry
    white wine
200 g/7 oz/1 cup caster sugar
175 ml/6 fl oz/¾ cup
    eau de vie

1 Poach the peach halves in the wine for about 15 minutes, until tender. Cover and set aside overnight.

2 Remove the peaches from the pan and strain the liquid through a coffee filter. Add the sugar and eau de vie and stir to dissolve the sugar.

3 Pour the wine into clean, dry sterilized bottles, seal and label. Store in the fridge and drink within 2 weeks. Serve well chilled.

Sloe Gin

This is a real country drink, which was traditionally used to celebrate high days and holidays.

Makes 750 ml/1¼ pints/3 cups

INGREDIENTS
450 g/1 lb/12 cups sloes
75–115 g/3–4 oz/⅓–½ cup caster sugar
750 ml/1¼ pints/3 cups gin

1 Wash the sloes and remove any stalks, twigs or leaves. Prick each sloe all over with a toothpick or needle, then pack the fruit into a wide-necked jar or bottle.

2 Add caster sugar so that it comes halfway up the jar or bottle, then fill to the top with gin and seal. Leave in a dark place for about 3 months. Shake the jar from time to time to help the sugar dissolve.

3 When the gin is ready to bottle, strain off the sloes through muslin and decant the gin into a clean, dry, sterilized bottle. Seal and label.

COOK'S TIP: Some recipes for sloe gin recommend adding a few drops of almond flavouring along with the sugar. If you gather sloes after the first frosts, you will have the perfect Christmas present.

Right: Sloe Gin (left and front); Peach Wine

Tomato Chutney

This spicy chutney is delicious served with a selection of cheeses and biscuits, or to complement cold meats.

Makes 4 x 450 g/
1 lb jars

INGREDIENTS
900 g/2 lb tomatoes, peeled
225 g/8 oz/1⅓ cups raisins
225 g/8 oz onions, chopped
225 g/8 oz/generous 1 cup
  caster sugar
600 ml/1 pint/2½ cups
  malt vinegar

1 Chop the tomatoes roughly. Put them in a preserving pan. Add the raisins, onions and caster sugar and pour in the vinegar.

2 Bring to the boil and simmer for 2 hours, uncovered. Ladle the chutney into sterilized jars. Seal and label.

3 Store in a cool, dark place. The chutney will keep unopened for up to a year. Once opened, store in the fridge and consume within a week.

Mixed Fruit Chutney

This chutney makes the perfect accompaniment to cold meat, pâtés and cheese. It has a sweet, but spicy flavour.

Makes 1.8 kg/4 lb

INGREDIENTS
450 g/1 lb/9 plums, stoned
450 g/1 lb/6 pears, peeled
    and cored
225 g/8 oz/2 cooking apples, peeled
    and cored
225 g/8 oz/4 sticks celery
450 g/1 lb onions, sliced
450 g/1 lb tomatoes, peeled
115 g/4 oz/½ cup raisins
15 g/½ oz grated fresh
    root ginger
30 ml/2 tbsp pickling spice
900 ml/1½ pints/3¾ cups
    cider vinegar
450 g/1 lb/2¼ cups granulated sugar

1 Chop the plums, pears, apples, celery and onions and cut the tomatoes into quarters. Place all these ingredients with the raisins and ginger in a very large saucepan.

2 Place the pickling spice in a piece of muslin and tie with string to secure. Add to the saucepan with half the vinegar and bring to the boil, stirring occasionally. Cook for about 2 hours.

3 When all the ingredients are tender, stir in the remaining vinegar and the sugar. Boil until thick, remove the bag of spices and fill warm, sterilized dry jars with chutney. Cover and label when cold.

Apple & Mint Jelly

This jelly is delicious served with garden peas, as well as the more traditional rich roasted meats such as lamb.

Makes 3 x 450 g/1 lb jars

INGREDIENTS
900 g/2 lb Bramley cooking apples
granulated sugar
45 ml/3 tbsp chopped fresh mint

1 Chop the apples roughly and put them in a preserving pan. Add enough water to cover. Simmer until the fruit is soft.

2 Pour the apple mixture through a jelly bag, allowing it to drip over a bowl overnight. Do not squeeze the bag or the jelly will become cloudy.

3 Measure the amount of juice. To every 600 ml/1 pint/2½ cups of juice, you need to add 500 g/1¼ lb/2½ cups granulated sugar.

4 Place the juice and sugar in a large pan and heat gently. Dissolve the sugar and then bring to the boil. When setting point is reached, leave to cool.

5 Stir in the mint and ladle into sterilized jars. Seal and label. Store in a cool, dark place. The jelly will keep unopened for up to a year. Once opened, keep in the fridge and consume within a week.

Honey Mustard

This mustard is richly flavoured and delicious in sauces and dressings.

Makes about 500 g/1¼ lb/ 2 cups

INGREDIENTS
225 g/8 oz/1¾ cups white mustard seeds
15 ml/1 tbsp ground cinnamon
2.5 ml/½ tsp ground ginger
300 ml/½ pint/1¼ cups white
   wine vinegar
90 ml/6 tbsp clear
   dark honey

1 Put the mustard seeds in a bowl and stir in the ground cinnamon and ginger. Pour in the white wine vinegar and set the mixture aside in a cool place but not the fridge, covered with a dish towel or clear film, to soak overnight.

2 Transfer the mixture to a mortar and pound with a pestle, gradually adding the honey, until a smooth paste forms. Add a little extra vinegar if necessary.

3 Spoon the mustard into dry, sterilized jars, seal and label. Use within 4 weeks.

Right, from left: Honey Mustard;
Horseradish Mustard; Tarragon
Champagne Mustard

Horseradish Mustard

A tangy relish, this goes well with meats, smoked fish or cheese.

Makes about 400 g/ 14 oz/1¾ cups

INGREDIENTS
45 ml/3 tbsp white mustard seeds
250 ml/8 fl oz/1 cup boiling water
115 g/4 oz/1 cup dry mustard powder
115 g/4 oz/generous ½ cup sugar
120 ml/4 fl oz/½ cup white wine vinegar
50 ml/2 fl oz/¼ cup olive oil
5 ml/1 tsp lemon juice

FOR THE HORSERADISH SAUCE
45 ml/3 tbsp grated horseradish
15 ml/1 tbsp white wine vinegar
5 ml/1 tsp caster sugar
150 ml/¼ pint/⅔ cup double cream
salt

1 Place the mustard seeds in a bowl and pour in the boiling water. Set aside for 1 hour. Place the horseradish in a bowl and stir in the vinegar, sugar and a pinch of salt. Stir in the cream and set aside in the fridge.

2 Drain the mustard seeds and transfer to a food processor. Add the mustard powder, sugar, vinegar, oil, lemon juice and 30 ml/2 tbsp horseradish sauce. Process to a smooth paste. Spoon into dry, sterilized jars, cover and label. Store in the fridge and use within 3 months.

Tarragon Champagne Mustard

This delicately flavoured mustard is very good with cold seafood or chicken.

Makes about 250 g/9 oz/1 cup

INGREDIENTS
30 ml/2 tbsp white mustard seeds
75 ml/5 tbsp champagne vinegar
115 g/4 oz/1 cup dry
  mustard powder
115 g/4 oz/½ cup soft
  brown sugar
2.5 ml/½ tsp salt
50 ml/2 fl oz/¼ cup virgin olive oil
60 ml/4 tbsp chopped
  fresh tarragon

1 Put the mustard seeds in a bowl and pour in the vinegar. Set aside to soak overnight.

2 Pour the mustard seed mixture into a blender or food processor and add the mustard powder, sugar and salt. Process until smooth. With the motor still running, gradually add the oil. Stir in the tarragon.

3 Pour the mustard into dry, sterilized jars, seal and label. Store in a cool place.

Pickled Beetroot

Bake the beetroot first for a richer earthier flavour than the usual boiled beetroot.

Makes 450 g/1 lb

INGREDIENTS
450 g/1 lb beetroot, cooked
1 large onion, sliced
300 ml/½ pint/1¼ cups
   cider vinegar
150 ml/¼ pint/⅔ cup water
50 g/2 oz/¼ cup sugar
few strips of fresh
   horseradish (optional)

1 Slice the beetroot and pack it into a dry sterilized jar, layering it with the sliced onion.

2 Pour the vinegar and water into a saucepan. Add the sugar and horseradish, if using, and bring to the boil. Pour the liquid over the beetroot, seal and label. Store in a cool place and use within 1 month.

COOK'S TIP: Wash the beetroot before cooking, with the root, skin and a little stalk intact. This will prevent any juice from leaking out.

Right, clockwise from top left: Pickled Beetroot; Pickled Red Cabbage; Bottled Cherry Tomatoes

Pickled Red Cabbage

This pickle is good served with bread and cheese or cold meats such as duck or goose.

Makes 1–1.6 kg/2¼–3½ lb

INGREDIENTS
675 g/1½ lb shredded red cabbage
1 large Spanish onion, sliced
25 g/1 oz sea salt
600 ml/1 pint/2½ cups red wine vinegar
75 g/3 oz/generous ⅓ cup brown sugar
15 ml/1 tbsp coriander seeds
3 cloves
2.5 cm/1 in piece fresh root ginger
1 star anise
2 bay leaves
4 eating apples

1 Mix the cabbage, onion and salt in a colander and set aside to drain overnight. Rinse thoroughly and remove excess water with a cloth.

2 Pour the vinegar into a saucepan and add the sugar, coriander seeds, cloves, ginger, star anise and bay leaves. Bring to the boil. Then remove from the heat and allow to cool.

3 Core and chop the apples, then layer with the cabbage and onion in dry sterilized jars. Strain the vinegar, if wished, and pour into the jars. Seal and label. Store for 1 week before using and eat within 2 months.

Bottled Cherry Tomatoes

Sweetly delicious, cherry tomatoes bottled in their own juices with garlic and basil are a perfect accompaniment to ham.

Makes 1 kg/2¼ lb

INGREDIENTS

1 kg/2¼ lb cherry tomatoes
5 ml/1 tsp salt per 1 litre/1¾ pint/4 cup jar
5 ml/1 tsp sugar per 1 litre/1¾ pint/4 cup jar
fresh basil
5 garlic cloves per jar

1 Prick each tomato with a toothpick. Pack the tomatoes into dry, sterilized jars, adding the salt and sugar as you go.

2 Fill the jars to within 2 cm/¾ in of the top, tucking the basil and garlic among the tomatoes. Preheat the oven to 120°C/250°F/Gas ½. Rest the lids on the jars, but do not seal. Stand the jars on a baking tray lined with cardboard or newspaper in the oven for 45 minutes, or until simmering.

3 Remove the jars from the oven, seal and label. Store in a cool place and use within 6 months.

Peppers in Olive Oil

Their wonderful flavour and colour makes these peppers a lovely gift.

Makes 3 x 450 g/1 lb jars

INGREDIENTS
3 red peppers
3 yellow peppers
3 green peppers
300 ml/½ pint/1¼ cups olive oil
2.5 ml/½ tsp salt
2.5 ml/½ tsp freshly ground black pepper
3 thyme sprigs

1 Prepare a hot grill or preheat the oven to 200°C/400°F/Gas 6. Put the whole peppers on a grill rack or on a baking sheet. Place under the grill or in the oven and cook them for about 10 minutes, until the skins are charred and blistered all over. Turn frequently during cooking.

2 Allow the peppers to cool for at least 5 minutes, then peel off the skins. Remove the cores, seeds and stalks.

3 Slice each of the peppers thinly, keeping each colour separate, and place each into a separate dish.

4 Pour one-third of the olive oil over each of the peppers. Sprinkle with salt and pepper and add a sprig of thyme to each dish. Stir to blend well.

5 Fill three dry, sterilized jars with a mixture of peppers, or keep the colours separate. Top up each jar with the oil. Seal and label.

Hot Thai Pickled Shallots

Thai pink shallots require lengthy preparation, but they look exquisite.

Makes 2–3 jars

INGREDIENTS
–6 small red or green bird's eye chillies,
  halved and seeded, if liked
00 g/1¼ lb Thai pink shallots, peeled
 large garlic cloves, peeled, halved and
  green shoot removed

FOR THE VINEGAR
00 ml/1 pint/2½ cups cider vinegar
0 g/1½ oz/3 tbsp granulated sugar
0 ml/2 tsp salt
 cm/2 in piece fresh root ginger, sliced
5 ml/1 tbsp coriander seeds
 lemon grass stalks, cut in
  half lengthways
 kaffir lime leaves or strips of
  lime rind
5 ml/1 tbsp chopped fresh coriander

1 Prick whole (hotter) chillies several times with a cocktail stick. Bring a large pan of water to the boil. Blanch the chillies, shallots and garlic for 1–2 minutes, then drain. Rinse under cold water, then leave to drain.

2 Put all the vinegar ingredients except the fresh coriander in a pan and bring to the boil. Simmer over a low heat for 3–4 minutes, then cool.

3 Discard the ginger, then boil again. Add the fresh coriander, garlic and chillies. Cook for 1 minute and drain over a bowl. Pack the shallots into sterilized jars with the lemon grass, lime leaves, chillies and garlic. Pour in the vinegar. Cool, seal and leave in a dark place for 2 months before eating.

Savoury Butters

These unusual flavoured butters can be used as garnishes for meat, fish and vegetables, as a topping for canapés or as an addition to sauces.

Makes about 50 g/2 oz/¼ cup of each flavour

INGREDIENTS
450 g/1 lb/2 cups unsalted butter
25 g/1 oz/2 tbsp Stilton
3 anchovy fillets
5 ml/1 tsp curry paste
1 garlic clove, crushed
10 ml/2 tsp finely chopped fresh tarragon
15 ml/1 tbsp creamed horseradish
15 ml/1 tbsp chopped fresh parsley
5 ml/1 tsp grated lime rind
1.5 ml/¼ tsp chilli sauce

1 Place the butter in a food processor. Process until light and fluffy. Divide the butter into eight portions.

2 Crumble the Stilton and mix together with a portion of butter. Pound the anchovies to a paste in a mortar with a pestle and mix with the second portion of butter. Stir the curry paste into the third, and the crushed garlic into the fourth portion.

3 Stir the tarragon into the fifth portion and the creamed horseradish into the sixth portion. Add the parsley and the lime rind to the seventh portion, and add the chilli sauce to the last portion.

4 Pack each different kind of flavoured butter into a tiny sterilized jar and label. Store in the fridge.

Smoked Salmon Pâté

This luxury pâté makes a fine gift for a special person. Pack it in a pretty dish to give as part of the gift. Store in the fridge.

Makes 4 small ramekin dishes

INGREDIENTS

350 g/12 oz fresh salmon fillet
1.5 ml/¼ tsp salt
2.5 ml/½ tsp freshly ground
  black pepper
15 ml/1 tbsp chopped fresh dill,
  plus sprigs to garnish
115 g/4 oz/4 slices
  smoked salmon
115 g/4 oz/½ cup curd or
  cream cheese
75 g/3 oz/6 tbsp unsalted butter
50 g/2 oz/1 cup fresh
  white breadcrumbs
5 ml/1 tsp lemon juice
30 ml/2 tbsp Madeira

1 Preheat the oven to 190°C/375°F/ Gas 5. Put the salmon on a piece of greaseproof paper placed on top of a sheet of foil. Sprinkle with salt, pepper and dill. Seal the foil and place on a baking sheet. Bake for 10 minutes, or until just tender. Leave until cold, then remove the skin. Save any juices.

2 Cut out four pieces of smoked salmon to fit the bases of the four dishes. Cut out four strips to fit around the inside edges. Cover and chill.

3 Process the salmon, juices and remaining ingredients in a food processor until smooth. Press into the dishes and cover with more smoked salmon. Garnish, cover and chill.

A Quarter of Herby Cheeses

These cheeses make the perfect gift when you are invited out to dinner.

Makes 4 cheeses

INGREDIENTS
DILL & PINK PEPPERCORN CHEESE
150 g/5 oz mild medium-fat goat's cheese
4 fresh dill sprigs, finely chopped
2.5 ml/½ tsp crushed pink peppercorns

THYME & CHOPPED GARLIC CHEESE
100 g/3¾ oz round full-fat goat's cheese
4 thyme sprigs (leaves and flower pieces)
1 garlic clove, finely chopped

MINTED FETA
200 g/7 oz feta cheese
1 small bunch fresh mint, finely chopped

TARRAGON & LEMON CHEESE
225 g/8 oz low-fat soft or cream cheese
1 small bunch fresh tarragon, leaves
    finely chopped
coarsely grated rind of ½ lemon

1 For the dill and pink peppercorn cheese, place the cheese on a plate. Combine the dill and peppercorns. Press over the cheese with a spoon.

2 For the thyme and chopped garlic cheese, put the cheese on a plate. Press the thyme and garlic over the cheese with a spoon.

3 For the minted feta, drain the cheese and cut into small dice. Roll the dice in the mint until lightly coated.

4 For the tarragon and lemon cheese, put the cheese on a plate and cut into two squares. Lightly coat both pieces with tarragon and then with lemon rind. Wrap all the cheeses in waxed paper or non-stick baking paper, chill until required, and use within 3 days.

Thyme & Mustard Biscuits

These aromatic digestive-type biscuits are delicious served with cheese.

Makes about 40

INGREDIENTS
175 g/6 oz/1½ cups wholemeal flour
50 g/2 oz/½ cup medium oatmeal
30 ml/2 tbsp caster sugar
10 ml/2 tsp baking powder
30 ml/2 tbsp fresh thyme leaves
50 g/2 oz/4 tbsp butter
25 g/1 oz/2 tbsp white vegetable fat
45 ml/3 tbsp milk
10 ml/2 tsp Dijon mustard
30 ml/2 tbsp sesame seeds
salt and freshly ground black pepper

1 Preheat the oven to 200°C/400°F/ Gas 6. Put the flour, oatmeal, sugar, baking powder, thyme leaves and seasoning into a bowl and mix. Cut the fats into pieces and add to the bowl, then rub in to form fine crumbs.

2 Mix the milk and mustard together, stir into the flour mixture and continue mixing until you have a soft but not sticky dough.

3 Knead lightly on a floured surface, then roll out to a thickness of 5 mm/ ¼ in. Stamp out 5 cm/2 in rounds with a fluted biscuit cutter and arrange, spaced slightly apart, on two greased baking sheets. Reroll the trimmings and continue stamping out biscuits until all the dough is used.

4 Prick the biscuits with a fork and sprinkle with sesame seeds. Cook for 10–12 minutes, until lightly browned, alternating them on the oven shelves. Cool on the trays then pack into a small biscuit tin, or tie in cellophane bundles. Store for up to 5 days.

Herb-&-spice-flavoured Oils

Any good quality oil may be flavoured with herbs, spices, peppers, olives or anchovies. They look attractive in the kitchen, as well as being ready for use

Makes 300 ml/½ pint/1¼ cups of each flavour

INGREDIENTS
900 ml/1½ pints/3¾ cups olive,
    grapeseed or almond oil

HERB OIL
fresh sage, thyme, oregano, tarragon and
    rosemary sprigs
1 bay leaf sprig

SPICED OIL
30 ml/2 tbsp whole cloves
3 mace blades
15 ml/1 tbsp cardamom pods
15 ml/1 tbsp coriander seeds
3 dried chillies
1 bay sprig
2 lime slices
2 cinnamon sticks

MEDITERRANEAN OIL
2 mini red peppers
3 black olives
3 green olives
3 anchovy fillets
1 bay sprig
strip of lemon rind

*Opposite, from left: Herb Oil;
Spiced Oil; Mediterranean Oil*

1 Have ready three dry, sterilized bottles and corks. For the herb oil, place all the herb sprigs together and trim to fit inside the first bottle. Insert them stem by stem, short lengths first, and arrange them using a long skewer.

2 To make the spiced oil, add all the ingredients to the second bottle, using a funnel and a teaspoon for the smaller items.

3 For the Mediterranean oil, grill the peppers until tender, turning. Add to the third bottle with the other ingredients. Fill each bottle with oil and seal. Label and keep cool until required.

Chilli Oil

For a more robust flavour still, add garlic, thyme and peppercorns.

Makes 500 ml/17 fl oz/2¼ cups

INGREDIENTS
500 ml/17 fl oz/2¼ cups virgin olive oil
1 small fresh green chilli
5 small fresh red chillies

1 Fill a dry, sterilized bottle with the olive oil. Slice the green chilli crossways into thin rings and add with the whole red chillies to the oil.

2 Seal tightly and leave to infuse for 10–14 days. Shake occasionally.

Saffron Oil

Saffron has never been surpassed for its flavour and colour.

Makes 250 ml/8 fl oz/1 cup

INGREDIENTS
large pinch saffron strands
250 ml/8 fl oz/1 cup light olive oil or pure sunflower oil

Put the saffron strands in a dry, sterilized bottle. Fill the bottle with oil and seal. Leave to infuse for 2 weeks, gently shaking the bottle daily.

Opposite, from left: Chilli Oil; Saffron Oil; Garlic Oil

Garlic Oil

This oil is delicious in dressings and on fish, meat and vegetables.

Makes 750 ml/1¼ pints/3 cups

INGREDIENTS
900 ml/1½ pints/3¾ cups extra virgin olive oil
25 large plump garlic cloves, peeled

1 Heat the oil to a gentle simmer in a small pan, then add the garlic cloves and poach them for 25 minutes, or until tender and translucent. Leave in the saucepan until cool.

2 Strain the garlic cloves from the oil, reserving them for another use. Pour the oil into a sterilized bottle, seal, label and use within 10 days.

Rosemary Vinegar

Herb vinegars are excellent for adding flavour to a range of dressings and sauces.

Makes 600 ml/
1 pint/2½ cups

INGREDIENTS
600 ml/1 pint/2½ cups
  white wine or
  cider vinegar
90 ml/6 tbsp chopped fresh rosemary,
  plus some whole sprigs

1 Bring the vinegar to the boil in a saucepan, then pour it over the rosemary in a bowl. Cover and leave to infuse for 3 days.

2 Strain and pour it into a dry, sterilized bottle, adding a sprig of rosemary for decoration.

VARIATIONS: Try making flavoured vinegars from other fresh herbs as well as rosemary. Tarragon works particularly well; prepare tarragon vinegar in summer for the ideal winter gift.

Opposite, from left: Rosemary Vinegar; Raspberry Vinegar; Lemon & Lime Vinegar

Raspberry Vinegar

Fruit-flavoured vinegar gives a delicious depth to dressings and enhances the flavour of fruit.

Makes 750 ml/1¼ pints/3 cups strained vinegar

INGREDIENTS
600 ml/1 pint/2½ cups red wine vinegar
15 ml/1 tbsp pickling spice
450 g/1 lb raspberries, fresh or frozen
2 sprigs fresh lemon thyme

1 Pour the vinegar into a saucepan, add the pickling spice and heat gently for 5 minutes.

2 Pour the hot vinegar mixture over the raspberries in a bowl and then add the lemon thyme. Cover and leave to infuse for 2 days in a cool, dark place, stirring occasionally.

3 Remove the thyme and raspberries and strain the liquid. Pour the flavoured vinegar into a dry sterilized bottle, seal and label.

Lemon & Lime Vinegar

Citrus-flavoured vinegars are wonderful for adding to naturally piquant sauces such as hollandaise.

Makes 600 ml/
1 pint/2½ cups

INGREDIENTS
600 ml/1 pint/2½ cups white wine vinegar
rind of 1 lime
rind of 1 lemon

1 Bring the vinegar to the boil in a saucepan, then pour it over the lime and lemon rind in a bowl. Cover and leave to infuse for 3 days.

2 Strain and pour it into a dry sterilized bottle, adding fresh rind.

Rose Petal Vinegar

This vinegar may be used in a dressing for summer salads and it is also effective as a cool compress to ease a nagging headache.

Makes 300 ml/½ pint/1¼ cups

INGREDIENTS
scented red rose petals
300 ml/½ pint/1¼ cups
   good quality white
   wine vinegar

2 Snip off any blemished parts of the petals. Prepare enough petals to fill a cup and put them into a large glass jar or an attractive bottle.

1 Pull the rose petals from the flowerheads. Scald the vinegar by bringing it to just below boiling point and allow to cool.

COOK'S TIPS: Make sure that the rose petals have not been sprayed with pesticide. The best time to pick rose petals for culinary use is on a sunny day before 12 p.m. when their oil is at its most concentrated.

3 Add the cooled vinegar, cover the jar or bottle tightly and leave on a sunny windowsill for at least 3 weeks before using.

Glacé Fruits

Choose just one type of fruit, or select a variety if you prefer, such as cherries, plums, peaches, apricots, starfruit, pineapple, apples, oranges, lemons, limes and clementines.

Makes 24 pieces

INGREDIENTS
450 g/1 lb fruit
1 kg/2¼ lb/4½ cups granulated sugar
115 g/4 oz/1 cup powdered glucose

1 Remove the stones from cherries, plums, peaches and apricots. Peel and core pineapple and cut into cubes or rings. Peel, core and quarter apples and thinly slice citrus fruits. Prick the skins of cherries with a stainless steel needle so the syrup can penetrate the skin.

2 Place enough of the prepared fruit in a saucepan to cover the base, keeping individual types together. Add enough water to cover the fruit and simmer very gently, to avoid breaking it, until almost tender. Use a slotted spoon to lift the fruit and place in a shallow dish, removing any skins if necessary. Repeat until all the fruit has been cooked.

3 Measure 300 ml/½ pint/1¼ cups of the liquid, or make up this quantity with water if necessary. Pour into the saucepan and add 50 g/2 oz/4 tbsp of the sugar and the glucose. Heat gently, stirring occasionally, until dissolved. Bring to the boil and pour over the fruit in the dish, completely immersing it. Leave overnight.

4 Drain the syrup from the fruit into the saucepan and add another 50 g/2 oz/4 tbsp of the sugar. Heat gently to dissolve the sugar and bring to the boil. Pour the syrup over the fruit and leave overnight.

5 Repeat this process each day for five more days, each time draining off the syrup, dissolving 50 g/2 oz/4 tbsp of the sugar, boiling the syrup and then immersing the fruit again and leaving overnight.

6 Drain the fruit, dissolve a further 75 g/3 oz/⅓ cup of the sugar in the syrup and bring to the boil. Add the fruit to the syrup and cook gently for 3 minutes. Return to the dish and leave for another 2 days.

7 Repeat step 6; at this stage the syrup should look like clear honey. Leave in the dish for at least a further 10 days, or up to 3 weeks.

8 Place a wire rack over a tray and remove each piece of fruit with a slotted spoon. Arrange on the rack. Dry the fruit in a warm dry place or in the oven at the lowest setting until the surface no longer feels sticky. To coat in sugar, spear each piece of fruit and plunge into boiling water, then roll in granulated sugar.

9 To dip into syrup, place the remaining sugar and 175 ml/6 fl oz/ ¾ cup water in a saucepan. Heat gently until the sugar has dissolved, then boil for 1 minute. Dip each piece of fruit into boiling water, then quickly into the syrup. Place on the wire rack and leave in a warm place until dry. Place in paper cases and pack into boxes.

Marzipan Fruits

These eye-catching and realistic little fruits will make the perfect gift for people who love marzipan.

Makes 450 g/1 lb

INGREDIENTS
450 g/1 lb white marzipan
yellow, green, red, orange and burgundy
    food colouring dusts
30 ml/2 tbsp whole cloves

1 Cover a baking sheet with non-stick baking paper. Cut the marzipan into quarters. Take one piece and cut it into ten even-sized pieces. Place a little of each of the food colouring dusts into a palette, or place small amounts spaced apart on a plate. Cut two-thirds of the cloves into two pieces, making a stem and core end.

2 Taking the ten pieces, shape each one into a small, neat ball. Dip one ball into the yellow food colouring, dust off the excess, and roll between the palms of the hands to colour. Re-dip into the green colouring and re-roll to tint the balls a greeny-yellow colour.

3 Using your forefinger, roll one end of the ball to make a pear shape. Press a clove stem into the top and a core end into the base. Repeat the process with the remaining nine balls of marzipan. Place the pears on the baking sheet.

4 Cut another piece of the marzipan into ten pieces and shape into balls. Dip each piece into green food colouring dust and roll in the palms to colour evenly. Add a spot of red colouring dust and roll to blend the colour. Using a ball tool or the end of a paintbrush, indent the top and base to make an apple shape. Insert a stem and core.

5 Repeat the process described above using another piece of the marzipan to make a further ten orange coloured balls. Roll each over the surface of a fine grater to give the texture of an orange skin. Press a clove core into the base of each.

Take the remaining piece of marzipan, reserve a small piece, and mould the rest into lots of tiny marzipan beads. Colour them burgundy with the food colouring dust. Place a whole clove on the baking sheet. Arrange a cluster of burgundy beads in the shape of a bunch of grapes. Repeat with the remaining burgundy beads of marzipan to make another three bunches of grapes.

7 Roll out the remaining tiny piece of marzipan thinly and brush with green food colouring dust. Using a small vine leaf cutter, cut out eight leaves, mark the veins with a knife and place two on each bunch of grapes, bending to give a realistic appearance. When all the marzipan fruits are dry, pack into gift boxes.

Turkish Delight

Try different flavours, such as lemon, crème de menthe and orange, and vary the colours accordingly.

Makes 450 g/1 lb

INGREDIENTS
450 g/1 lb/2¼ cups granulated sugar
300 ml/½ pint/1¼ cups water
25 g/1 oz powdered gelatine
2.5 ml/½ tsp tartaric acid
30 ml/2 tbsp rose water
pink food colouring
45 ml/3 tbsp icing sugar, sifted
15 ml/1 tbsp cornflour

1 Wet the insides of two 18 cm/7 in shallow square tins with water. Place the sugar and all but 60 ml/4 tbsp of the water in a heavy-based pan. Heat gently, stirring occasionally, until the sugar has dissolved.

2 Blend the gelatine and remaining water in a small bowl and place over a saucepan of hot water. Stir occasionally until dissolved. Bring the sugar syrup to the boil and boil steadily for about 8 minutes, or until the syrup registers 127°C/260°F on a sugar thermometer.

3 Stir the tartaric acid into the gelatine, then pour into the boiling syrup and stir until well blended. Remove from the heat.

4 Add the rose water and a few drops of pink food colouring to tint the mixture pale pink. Pour the mixture into the tins and allow to set for several hours or overnight.

5 Dust a sheet of greaseproof paper with some of the icing sugar and cornflour. Dip the base of the tin in hot water. Invert on to the paper. Cut into 2.5 cm/1 in squares using an oiled knife. Toss in the icing sugar mixture to coat evenly.

COOK'S TIP: If you are not giving the Turkish Delight away immediately, it may be stored in an airtight container lined with greaseproof paper.

Coffee Chocolate Truffles

Because these classic chocolates contain fresh cream, they should be stored in the fridge and eaten within a few days.

Makes 24

INGREDIENTS
350 g/12 oz plain chocolate
75 ml/5 tbsp double cream
30 ml/2 tbsp coffee liqueur, such as
   Tia Maria, Kahlúa or Toussaint
115 g/4 oz good quality white
   dessert chocolate
115 g/4 oz good quality milk
   dessert chocolate

1 Melt 225 g/8 oz of the plain chocolate in a bowl over a pan of barely simmering water. Stir in the cream and liqueur, then chill the mixture in the fridge for 4 hours, until it is firm.

2 Divide the mixture into 24 equal pieces and quickly roll each into a ball. Chill the chocolate balls in the fridge for one more hour, or until they are firm again.

3 Melt the remaining plain, white and milk chocolate in separate small bowls. Using two forks, carefully dip eight of the truffles, one at a time, into the melted milk chocolate.

4 Dip eight more truffles in the white chocolate and then the rest of the truffles in the plain chocolate. Place the truffles on a board, covered with wax paper or foil. Leave them to set before removing and wrapping.

VARIATIONS: Ring the changes if you like by adding one of the following ingredients to the basic truffle mixture:
Ginger – Stir in 40 g/1½ oz/¼ cup finely chopped crystallized ginger.
Candied fruit – Stir in 50 g/2 oz/ ⅓ cup finely chopped candied fruit, such as pineapple and orange.
Pistachio – Stir in 25 g/1 oz/¼ cup chopped skinned pistachio nuts.
Hazelnut – Roll each ball of chilled truffle mixture around a whole skinned hazelnut.
Raisin – Soak 40 g/1½ oz/generous ¼ cup raisins overnight in 15 ml/ 1 tbsp coffee liqueur, such as Tia Maria or Kahlúa, and stir into the truffle mixture.

Creamy Fudge

A good selection of fudge always makes a most welcome change from chocolates. Mix and match the flavours to make a gift-wrapped assortment.

Makes 900 g/2 lb

INGREDIENTS
50 g/2 oz/4 tbsp unsalted butter, plus extra
    for greasing
450 g/1 lb/2¼ cups granulated sugar
300 ml/½ pint/1¼ cups double cream
150 ml/¼ pint/⅔ cup milk
45 ml/3 tbsp water (this can be replaced
    with orange, apricot or cherry brandy,
    or strong coffee)
icing sugar or melted chocolate, to
    decorate (optional)

FLAVOURINGS
225 g/8 oz/1 cup plain or milk chocolate dots
115 g/4 oz/1 cup chopped almonds,
    hazelnuts, walnuts or Brazil nuts
115 g/4 oz/½ cup chopped glacé cherries,
    dates or dried apricots

1 Butter a 20 cm/8 in shallow square tin. Place the sugar, cream, butter, milk and water or other flavouring into a large heavy-based saucepan. Heat very gently, stirring occasionally using a long-handled wooden spoon, until all the sugar has completely dissolved.

2 Bring the mixture to the boil and boil steadily, stirring only occasionally to prevent the mixture from burning over the base of the saucepan. Boil until the fudge reaches just under "soft ball" stage: 113°C/235°F for a soft fudge.

3 If you are making chocolate-flavoured fudge, add the chocolate at this stage. Remove from the heat and beat thoroughly until the mixture starts to thicken and become opaque.

4 Just before this consistency has been reached, add chopped nuts for a nutty fudge, or glacé cherries or dried fruit for a fruit-flavoured fudge. Beat well until evenly blended.

5 Pour into the tin, taking care as the mixture is exceedingly hot. Leave until cool and almost set. Using a sharp knife, mark into small squares and leave in the tin until quite firm.

6 Turn the fudge out on to a board and turn over. Using a long-bladed knife, cut into neat squares. You can dust some of the pieces with icing sugar and drizzle others with melted chocolate if you like.

Cranberry Fudge

This rich candy comes from Scotland. You can use chopped pecans, crystallized ginger or other candied fruits instead if you like.

Makes about 1.2 kg/2½ lb

INGREDIENTS
115 g/4 oz/¼ cup fresh cranberries
900 g/2 lb/4 cups granulated sugar
50 g/2 oz/4 tbsp unsalted butter
175 ml/6 fl oz/¾ cup milk
15 ml/1 tbsp golden syrup
200 g/7 oz can condensed milk

1 Wash the cranberries, discarding any that are bruised or discoloured. Pat dry and set aside. Grease a 28 x 18 cm/11 x 7 in Swiss roll tin. Place the sugar, butter, milk and golden syrup in a heavy-based saucepan and bring to the boil over a low heat, stirring constantly.

2 Add the condensed milk, return to the boil and boil for 20 minutes more, stirring continuously, until the mixture reaches 125°C/257°F on a sugar thermometer, or until a spoonful of the mixture, dropped into a cup of cold water, sets hard.

3 Remove the saucepan from the heat and stir in the cranberries. Pour the mixture into the prepared tin and leave to set. Mark the fudge into squares just before it hardens.

4 When the fudge is completely cold, cut it into squares, using a heavy kitchen knife, and then store it in an airtight container.

Rose Petal Truffles

These glamorous chocolates are fun to make as a Valentine gift or for an engagement or wedding present.

Makes about 20

INGREDIENTS
500 g/1¼ lb plain chocolate
300 ml/½ pint/1¼ cups double cream
15 ml/1 tbsp rose water
2 drops rose essential oil
250 g/9 oz plain chocolate,
    for coating
crystallized rose petals, for decoration

1 Break the chocolate into a bowl or into the top of a double boiler. Add the double cream and set over a pan of barely simmering water. Heat gently, stirring constantly, until the chocolate has melted.

2 Mix in the rose water and essential oil, then pour into a baking tin lined with non-stick baking paper.

3 When cool and almost firm, take teaspoonfuls of the chocolate and shape into balls, using your hands. Chill the truffles until they are hard.

4 Melt the chocolate for the coating over a pan of simmering water. Skewer a truffle and dip it into the melted chocolate. Decorate with a crystallized rose petal before the chocolate has set, then leave on a sheet of non-stick baking paper to dry completely. Scatter with crystallized rose petals.

Stuffed Prunes

Chocolate-covered prunes, soaked in liqueur, hide a melt-in-the-mouth coffee and cream filling.

Makes about 30

INGREDIENTS
225 g/8 oz/1 cup unstoned prunes
50 ml/2 fl oz/¼ cup Armagnac
30 ml/2 tbsp ground coffee
150 ml/¼ pint/⅔ cup
   double cream
350 g/12 oz plain chocolate,
   broken into squares
10 g/¼ oz/½ tbsp vegetable fat
30 ml/2 tbsp cocoa powder,
   for dusting

1 Put the prunes in a bowl and pour the Armagnac over. Stir, then cover with clear film and set aside for 2 hours, or until the prunes have absorbed the liquid.

2 Use a sharp knife to make a slit along each prune to remove the stone, making a hollow for the filling, but leaving the fruit intact.

3 Put the coffee and cream in a pan and heat almost to boiling point. Cover, leave to infuse for 4 minutes, then heat again until almost boiling. Put 115 g/4 oz of the chocolate into a bowl and pour in the coffee cream through a sieve.

4 Stir until the chocolate has melted and the mixture is smooth. Leave to cool, until it has the consistency of softened butter.

5 Use a piping bag with a small plain nozzle and fill with the chocolate and coffee mixture. Pipe into the cavities of the prunes. Leave to chill in the fridge for 20 minutes.

VARIATION: Fresh dates can be used instead of prunes, if preferred.

6 Melt the remaining chocolate and vegetable fat in a bowl over a pan of hot water. Using a fork, dip the prunes one at a time into the chocolate to give them a generous coating. Place on non-stick baking paper to harden. Dust each with a little cocoa powder.

Chocolate Fruit & Nut Cookies

These simple, chunky gingerbread biscuits make a delicious gift, especially when presented in a decorative gift box.

Makes about 20

INGREDIENTS
225 g/8 oz plain chocolate
50 g/2 oz/¼ cup caster sugar
75 ml/2½ fl oz/⅓ cup water
75 g/3 oz/½ cup glacé cherries
40 g/1½ oz/scant ½ cup walnut halves
115 g/4 oz/1 cup whole
   blanched almonds

FOR THE GINGERBREAD
115 g/4 oz/½ cup unsalted
   butter, softened
115 g/4 oz/½ cup light muscovado sugar
1 egg, beaten
115 g/4 oz/⅓ cup treacle
400 g/14 oz/3½ cups self-raising flour
5 ml/1 tsp ground ginger
2.5 ml/½ tsp ground cloves
1.5 ml/¼ tsp chilli powder

1 First make the gingerbread. Cream the butter and sugar together until pale and fluffy. Beat in the egg and treacle. Sift the flour, ginger, cloves and chilli powder into the bowl. Using a wooden spoon, gradually mix the ingredients together to make a stiff paste. Turn out on to a lightly floured surface and knead lightly until smooth. Shape into a roll 20 cm/8 in long, wrap and chill for 30 minutes.

2 Preheat the oven to 180°C/350°F/ Gas 4. Grease two baking sheets. Cut the dough into 20 slices and space them on the baking sheets. Bake for 10 minutes. Leave on the baking sheets for 5 minutes and then transfer to a wire rack and leave to cool.

3 Break the chocolate into pieces. Put the sugar in a small, heavy-based saucepan with the water. Heat gently until the sugar dissolves. Bring to the boil and boil for 1 minute, until slightly syrupy. Leave for 3 minutes to cool slightly and then stir in the chocolate until it has melted and made a smooth sauce.

4 Place the wire rack of biscuits over a large tray or board to catch the drips. Spoon a little of the melted chocolate mixture over the gingerbread biscuits, spreading it to the edges with the back of the spoon.

5 Cut the glacé cherries into small wedges. Gently press a walnut half into the centre of each biscuit. Arrange pieces of glacé cherry and almonds alternately around the walnuts. Leave to set in a cool place. Stack the biscuits in a pretty box or tin, lined with tissue paper, or tie in cellophane bundles.

Chocolate Boxes

These tiny chocolate boxes make the perfect containers for hand-made chocolates or sweets. Use white or milk chocolate with dark trimmings to vary the theme.

Makes 4

INGREDIENTS
225 g/8 oz plain or milk
   chocolate, melted
50 g/2 oz white chocolate

FOR THE DECORATION
hand-made chocolates or sweets,
   to fill
2 m/2 yd ribbon,
   1 cm/½ in wide

1 Line a large baking sheet with non-stick baking paper. Remove the bowl of melted chocolate from the heat and wipe the condensation off the base.

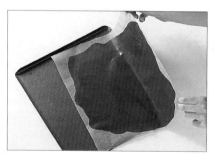

2 Pour all but 15 ml/1 tbsp of the chocolate over the baking paper and quickly spread to the edges using a palette knife. Pick up two corners of the paper and drop; do this several times on each side to level the surface of the chocolate.

3 Leave the chocolate until almost set but still pliable. Place a clean piece of non-stick baking paper on the surface, then invert the chocolate sheet and peel the paper away from the back of the chocolate.

4 Using a ruler and a scalpel or sharp knife, measure and cut the chocolate sheet into 16 5 x 5 cm/2 x 2 in squares to form the sides of the boxes. Measure and cut out eight 5.5 x 5.5 cm/2¼ x 2¼ in squares for the lids and bases of each of the chocolate boxes.

5 To assemble the boxes, paint a little of the remaining melted chocolate around the edges of one of the larger chocolate squares using a fine brush. Carefully place the side pieces of the boxes in position one at a time on the base. Brush the side edges and join the four squares together to form a box. Leave to set. Repeat to make the remaining three boxes.

6 Melt the white chocolate and spoon into a greaseproof paper piping bag. Fold down the top and snip off the point. Pipe 20 chocolate loops on to baking paper and leave to set. Decorate the sides of the boxes with chocolate loops, each secured with a bead of white chocolate. Alternatively, wrap a ribbon around each box and tie a bow, after filling the boxes.

This edition is published by Southwater

Southwater is an imprint of
Anness Publishing Ltd
Hermes House
88–89 Blackfriars Road
London SE1 8HA
tel. 020 7401 2077
fax 020 7633 9499

Distributed in the USA by
Anness Publishing Inc.
27 West 20th Street
Suite 504, New York NY 10011

Distributed in the UK by
The Manning Partnership
251–253 London Road East
Batheaston
Bath BA1 7RL
tel. 01225 852 727
fax 01225 852 852

Distributed in Australia by
Sandstone Publishing
Unit 1, 360 Norton Street, Leichhardt
New South Wales 2040
tel. 02 9560 7888
fax 02 9560 7488

Publisher: Joanna Lorenz
Editor: Valerie Ferguson
Series Designer: Bobbie Colgate Stone
Designer: Andrew Heath
Production Controller: Joanna King

Recipes contributed by: Catherine Atkinson,
Kathy Brown, Patrizia Diemling,
Stephanie Donaldson, Joanna Farrow,
Brian Glover, Sara Lewis, Janice Murfitt,
Katherine Richmond, Liz Trigg,
Elizabeth Wolf-Cohen.

Photography: Edward Allwright, Louise Dare,
John Freeman, Michelle Garrett,
William Lingwood, Polly Wreford.

1 3 5 7 9 10 8 6 4 2

Notes:

For all recipes, quantities are given in both metric and imperial measures and, where appropriate, measures are also given in standard cups and spoons.
Follow one set, but not a mixture, because they are not interchangeable.

Standard spoon and cup measures are level.

1 tsp = 5 ml   1 tbsp = 15 ml

1 cup = 250 ml/8 fl oz

Australian standard tablespoons are 20 ml. Australian readers should use 3 tsp in place of 1 tbsp for measuring small quantities of gelatine, cornflour, salt etc.

Medium eggs are used unless otherwise stated.